MILEAGE LOG

MAKE:		MODEL:		YEAR:
DATE:	ODOMETER: START | END		TOTAL:	DESTINATION / PURPOSE:

MILEAGE LOG

MAKE:		MODEL:		YEAR:
DATE:	ODOMETER: START | END		TOTAL:	DESTINATION / PURPOSE:

MILEAGE LOG

MAKE:		MODEL:		YEAR:
DATE:	ODOMETER: START | END		TOTAL:	DESTINATION / PURPOSE:

MILEAGE LOG

MAKE:		MODEL:		YEAR:
DATE:	ODOMETER: START | END		TOTAL:	DESTINATION / PURPOSE:

MILEAGE LOG

MAKE:		MODEL:		YEAR:
DATE:	**ODOMETER: START**	**END**	**TOTAL:**	**DESTINATION / PURPOSE:**

MILEAGE LOG

MAKE:		MODEL:		YEAR:
DATE:	ODOMETER: START | END		TOTAL:	DESTINATION / PURPOSE:

MILEAGE LOG

MAKE:		MODEL:		YEAR:
DATE:	ODOMETER: START	END		TOTAL:	DESTINATION / PURPOSE:

MILEAGE LOG

MAKE:		MODEL:		YEAR:
DATE:	ODOMETER: START | END		TOTAL:	DESTINATION / PURPOSE:

MILEAGE LOG

MAKE:		MODEL:		YEAR:
DATE:	ODOMETER: START | END		TOTAL:	DESTINATION / PURPOSE:

MILEAGE LOG

MAKE:		MODEL:		YEAR:
DATE:	ODOMETER: START | END		TOTAL:	DESTINATION / PURPOSE:

MILEAGE LOG

MAKE:		MODEL:		YEAR:
DATE:	**ODOMETER: START | END**		**TOTAL:**	**DESTINATION / PURPOSE:**

MILEAGE LOG

MAKE:		**MODEL:**		**YEAR:**
DATE:	**ODOMETER: START | END**		**TOTAL:**	**DESTINATION / PURPOSE:**

MILEAGE LOG

MAKE:		MODEL:		YEAR:
DATE:	**ODOMETER: START**	**END**	**TOTAL:**	**DESTINATION / PURPOSE:**

MILEAGE LOG

MAKE:		MODEL:		YEAR:
DATE:	ODOMETER: START | END		TOTAL:	DESTINATION / PURPOSE:

MILEAGE LOG

MAKE:		MODEL:		YEAR:
DATE:	ODOMETER: START | END		TOTAL:	DESTINATION / PURPOSE:

MILEAGE LOG

MAKE:		MODEL:		YEAR:
DATE:	ODOMETER: START | END		TOTAL:	DESTINATION / PURPOSE:

MILEAGE LOG

MAKE:		MODEL:		YEAR:
DATE:	ODOMETER: START | END		TOTAL:	DESTINATION / PURPOSE:

MILEAGE LOG

MAKE:		MODEL:		YEAR:
DATE:	ODOMETER: START | END		TOTAL:	DESTINATION / PURPOSE:

MILEAGE LOG

MAKE:		MODEL:		YEAR:
DATE:	ODOMETER: START | END		TOTAL:	DESTINATION / PURPOSE:

MILEAGE LOG

MAKE:		MODEL:		YEAR:
DATE:	ODOMETER: START | END		TOTAL:	DESTINATION / PURPOSE:

MILEAGE LOG

MAKE:		MODEL:		YEAR:
DATE:	ODOMETER: START | END		TOTAL:	DESTINATION / PURPOSE:

MILEAGE LOG

MAKE:		MODEL:		YEAR:
DATE:	ODOMETER: START | END		TOTAL:	DESTINATION / PURPOSE:

MILEAGE LOG

MAKE:		MODEL:		YEAR:
DATE:	ODOMETER: START | END		TOTAL:	DESTINATION / PURPOSE:

MILEAGE LOG

MAKE:		MODEL:		YEAR:
DATE:	ODOMETER: START |	END	TOTAL:	DESTINATION / PURPOSE:

MILEAGE LOG

MAKE:		MODEL:		YEAR:
DATE:	ODOMETER: START | END		TOTAL:	DESTINATION / PURPOSE:

MILEAGE LOG

MAKE:		MODEL:		YEAR:
DATE:	ODOMETER: START | END		TOTAL:	DESTINATION / PURPOSE:

MILEAGE LOG

MAKE:		MODEL:		YEAR:
DATE:	ODOMETER: START | END		TOTAL:	DESTINATION / PURPOSE:

MILEAGE LOG

MAKE:		MODEL:		YEAR:
DATE:	ODOMETER: START | END		TOTAL:	DESTINATION / PURPOSE:

MILEAGE LOG

MAKE:		MODEL:		YEAR:
DATE:	ODOMETER: START | END		TOTAL:	DESTINATION / PURPOSE:

MILEAGE LOG

MAKE:		MODEL:		YEAR:
DATE:	ODOMETER: START | END		TOTAL:	DESTINATION / PURPOSE:

MILEAGE LOG

MAKE:		MODEL:		YEAR:
DATE:	ODOMETER: START | END		TOTAL:	DESTINATION / PURPOSE:

MILEAGE LOG

MAKE:		MODEL:		YEAR:
DATE:	ODOMETER: START | END		TOTAL:	DESTINATION / PURPOSE:

MILEAGE LOG

MAKE:		MODEL:		YEAR:
DATE:	ODOMETER: START | END		TOTAL:	DESTINATION / PURPOSE:

MILEAGE LOG

MAKE:		MODEL:		YEAR:
DATE:	ODOMETER: START | END		TOTAL:	DESTINATION / PURPOSE:

MILEAGE LOG

MAKE:		MODEL:		YEAR:
DATE:	ODOMETER: START | END		TOTAL:	DESTINATION / PURPOSE:

MILEAGE LOG

MAKE:		MODEL:		YEAR:
DATE:	ODOMETER: START | END		TOTAL:	DESTINATION / PURPOSE:

MILEAGE LOG

MAKE:		MODEL:		YEAR:
DATE:	ODOMETER: START | END		TOTAL:	DESTINATION / PURPOSE:

MILEAGE LOG

MAKE:		MODEL:		YEAR:
DATE:	**ODOMETER: START | END**		**TOTAL:**	**DESTINATION / PURPOSE:**

MILEAGE LOG

MAKE:		MODEL:		YEAR:
DATE:	ODOMETER: START	END	TOTAL:	DESTINATION / PURPOSE:

MILEAGE LOG

MAKE:		MODEL:		YEAR:
DATE:	ODOMETER: START | END		TOTAL:	DESTINATION / PURPOSE:

MILEAGE LOG

MAKE:	MODEL:	YEAR:

DATE:	ODOMETER: START	END	TOTAL:	DESTINATION / PURPOSE:

MILEAGE LOG

MAKE:		MODEL:		YEAR:
DATE:	ODOMETER: START | END		TOTAL:	DESTINATION / PURPOSE:

MILEAGE LOG

MAKE:		MODEL:		YEAR:
DATE:	ODOMETER: START | END		TOTAL:	DESTINATION / PURPOSE:

MILEAGE LOG

MAKE:		MODEL:		YEAR:
DATE:	ODOMETER: START | END		TOTAL:	DESTINATION / PURPOSE:

MILEAGE LOG

MAKE:		MODEL:		YEAR:
DATE:	ODOMETER: START | END		TOTAL:	DESTINATION / PURPOSE:

MILEAGE LOG

MAKE:	MODEL:	YEAR:

DATE:	ODOMETER: START	END	TOTAL:	DESTINATION / PURPOSE:

MILEAGE LOG

MAKE:		MODEL:		YEAR:
DATE:	ODOMETER: START	END		TOTAL:	DESTINATION / PURPOSE:

MILEAGE LOG

MAKE:		MODEL:		YEAR:
DATE:	ODOMETER: START | END		TOTAL:	DESTINATION / PURPOSE:

MILEAGE LOG

MAKE:		MODEL:		YEAR:
DATE:	**ODOMETER: START | END**		**TOTAL:**	**DESTINATION / PURPOSE:**

MILEAGE LOG

MAKE:		MODEL:		YEAR:
DATE:	ODOMETER: START | END		TOTAL:	DESTINATION / PURPOSE:

MILEAGE LOG

MAKE:		MODEL:		YEAR:
DATE:	ODOMETER: START | END		TOTAL:	DESTINATION / PURPOSE:

MILEAGE LOG

MAKE:		MODEL:		YEAR:
DATE:	ODOMETER: START | END		TOTAL:	DESTINATION / PURPOSE:

MILEAGE LOG

MAKE:		MODEL:		YEAR:
DATE:	**ODOMETER: START | END**		**TOTAL:**	**DESTINATION / PURPOSE:**

MILEAGE LOG

MAKE:		MODEL:		YEAR:
DATE:	**ODOMETER: START**	**END**	**TOTAL:**	**DESTINATION / PURPOSE:**

MILEAGE LOG

MAKE:		MODEL:		YEAR:
DATE:	ODOMETER: START | END		TOTAL:	DESTINATION / PURPOSE:

MILEAGE LOG

MAKE:		MODEL:		YEAR:
DATE:	ODOMETER: START | END		TOTAL:	DESTINATION / PURPOSE:

MILEAGE LOG

MAKE:		MODEL:		YEAR:
DATE:	ODOMETER: START | END		TOTAL:	DESTINATION / PURPOSE:

MILEAGE LOG

MAKE:		**MODEL:**		**YEAR:**
DATE:	**ODOMETER: START | END**		**TOTAL:**	**DESTINATION / PURPOSE:**

MILEAGE LOG

MAKE:		MODEL:		YEAR:
DATE:	ODOMETER: START | END		TOTAL:	DESTINATION / PURPOSE:

MILEAGE LOG

MAKE:		MODEL:		YEAR:
DATE:	ODOMETER: START | END		TOTAL:	DESTINATION / PURPOSE:

www.ingramcontent.com/pod-product-compliance
Lightning Source LLC
LaVergne TN
LVHW021052100526
838202LV00083B/5742
* 9 7 8 3 7 4 9 7 2 8 1 3 8 *